Chemicals
in Action

Metals

Chris Oxlade

Heinemann Library
Chicago, Illinois

Designed by Tinstar Design
Illustrations by Jeff Edwards
Originated by Ambassador Litho
Printed in China

06 05 04
10 9 8 7 6 5 4 3

Library of Congress Cataloging-in-Publication Data
Oxlade, Chris.
     Metals / Chris Oxlade.
          p. cm. -- (Chemicals in action)
     Summary: Provides an introduction to metals, including their physical properties, their place in the periodic table, their uses in everyday life, and how they react with other substances. Includes experiments. Includes bibliographical references and index.
     ISBN 1-4034-2500-0 (lib. bdg.)
     1. Metals--Juvenile literature. [1. Metals.] I. Title.
     QD171 .O97 2002
     546'.31--dc21
                         2002004762

Acknowledgments
The author and publishers are grateful to the following for permission to reproduce copyright material: pp. 4, 5, 6, 10, 12, 15, 19, 24, 33, 35, 37 Science Photo Library; pp. 9, 16, 18, 28, 36, 39 Robert Harding; pp. 11, 13, 19, 25, 29 Trevor Clifford; p. 15 Holt Studios; pp. 17, 38 Roger Scruton; p. 22 Peter Gould; pp. 20, 26, 32 Andrew Lambert; p. 31 Telegraph Colour Library; p. 34 Paul Brierly.

Cover photograph: Photodisc.

The publishers would like to thank Ted Dolter and Dr. Nigel Saunders for their assistance in the preparation of this book.

Every effort has been made to contact copyright holders of any material reproduced in this book. Any omissions will be rectified in subsequent printings if notice is given to the publisher.

Some words are shown in bold, **like this.** You can find out what they mean by looking in the glossary.

Contents

Chemicals in Action

What's the link between an artificial joint, a jet engine, a computer, a battery, and a frying pan? The answer is **metals.** All these things are made of metals or work because of metals, or because of **chemical reactions** between metals. Our knowledge of how metals behave is used in choosing which metals to use in manufacturing, in engineering, in medicine, and in recycling.

The study of metals is part of the science of chemistry. Many people think of chemistry as something that scientists study by doing experiments in laboratories with special equipment. This part of chemistry is very important. It is how scientists find out what substances are made of and how they make new materials—but this is only a tiny part of chemistry. Most chemistry happens away from laboratories, in factories and chemical plants. Chemistry is used to manufacture an enormous range of items, such as synthetic fibers for fabrics, drugs to treat diseases, explosives for fireworks, solvents for paints, and fertilizers for growing crops.

The light, strong metal aluminum w used to make fuel tanks fo the Arianne *rocket.*

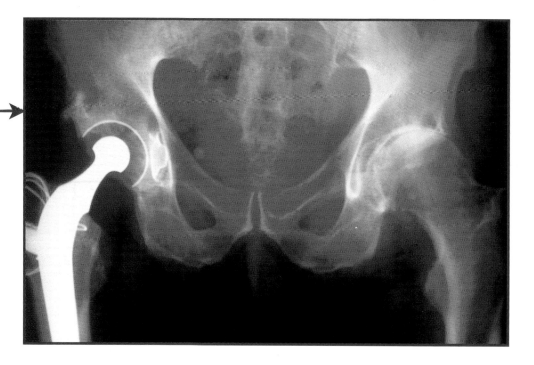

This **X-ray** shows an artificial ball-and-socket hip joint, made from metal that resists **corrosion.**

About the experiments

There are several experiments in the book for you to try. They will help you to understand some of the chemistry in the book. An experiment is designed to help solve a scientific problem. A scientist first develops a hypothesis, which might be the answer to the problem, then designs an experiment to test the hypothesis. She then observes the results of the experiment and concludes whether or not the results show the hypothesis to be correct. We know what we do about chemistry because scientists have carried out millions of experiments over hundreds of years. Experiments have helped us to understand why different substances have the **properties** they do. They have allowed scientists to discover many different metals, observe how metals behave in chemical reactions, and learn how to **extract** metals from the rocks of Earth's crust.

Doing the experiments

All the experiments in this book have been designed for you to do at home with everyday substances and equipment. They can also be done in a school laboratory. Always follow the safety advice given with each activity, and ask an adult to help you when the instructions tell you to.

About Metals

When you hear the word **"metal,"** you probably think of something shiny and hard, such as knives and forks, jewelry, pots and pans, and tools. Metals that are useful in making objects like these have special **properties.** For example, many metals are strong, have high **melting points,** and can **conduct** electricity. Metals are also used on a much bigger scale: they make up structures such as skyscrapers and bridges, and machines such as trains and trucks.

Metals are found in rocks that make up Earth's crust. Getting them out of the rocks and preparing them so that manufacturers can use them to make objects is a huge industry. Various **chemical reactions** are used to **extract** the metals from the rocks that contain them. Other chemical reactions change the metals when we use them. For example, some metals, such as iron, are weakened when they react with gases in the air.

The fuselages and wings of airplanes are made from aluminum. Some parts are made from strong aluminum alloys.

Metal elements

Metals used in metal objects are either pure metals or **alloys.** Pure metals contain only one sort of metal. Alloys contain a metal mixed with one or more other metals or **nonmetals.** When chemists talk about a metal, they mean a metal that is an **element**—a substance made up of just one type of **atom.** For example, the metal aluminum is made up of just aluminum atoms.

Metals are one of the two main types of elements, and they appear toward the left side of the periodic table. About three-quarters of all the elements are metals, and they are identified by their properties, such as their shininess and ability to conduct electricity. Most of the remaining elements are nonmetals A few elements have some of the properties of both metals and nonmetals. They are called **metalloids** or semimetals.

Most coins are made from durable alloys so that they will last a long time in circulation.

Alloys

An alloy is a material that is made up of a **mixture** of two or more different metals, or a metal and one or more nonmetals. They are made in chemical plants. Mixing different metals and nonmetals produces alloys that have useful properties. For example, brass—an alloy of copper and zinc—is stronger than either metal on its own. It also does not **corrode.**

Properties of Metals

There are more than a hundred different **elements,** and each has **properties** that make it look, feel, and behave differently from the others. Each one is made up of a different type of **atom.**

The elements are divided into two main types, **metals** and **nonmetals,** according to their properties. About three-quarters of the elements are metals. They all have similar properties to each other and they are described as metallic. They look and behave in a similar way. Nonmetals are elements that do not have the properties of metals.

This table shows the properties of metals and nonmetals:

Metals	Nonmetals
Mostly solids	Mostly gases at room temperature
Hard, shiny, and **malleable**	Weak, dull, and brittle when solids
Good **conductors** of electricity	Insulators (except graphite)
Good conductors of heat	Poor conductors of heat
Most have high **melting** and **boiling points**	Most have low melting and boiling points
High **densities**	Low densities
Oxides are **basic**	Oxides are **acidic**

Inside a metal

All materials are made up of incredibly tiny **particles,** called atoms, that are too small to see, even with the most powerful microscopes. An atom is made up of a central **nucleus** surrounded by particles called **electrons.** Each atom is attached to the atoms around it by chemical **bonds.** In a piece of metal, the atoms are arranged in neat rows and columns, and they are tightly packed together. This is why most metals are strong materials.

We make use of the properties of metals in structures such as bridges and skyscrapers. The frame of this bridge tower is made of strong metal girders, while the roadway is supported by strong, but flexible, cables.

Shine and color

All metals have shiny surfaces when they are freshly cut or polished. Many metals lose their shininess after a while because the metal at the surface reacts with oxygen in the air, forming a layer of oxide. Some metals, such as gold, do not react with oxygen—they stay shiny and are used for decorations such as jewelry. Most metals are gray or silvery in color.

Changing shape

Metals are flexible, meaning that they can change shape slightly and return to their original shape. This is why springs are made of metal. Metals are also **malleable,** so that a piece of metal can be hammered into a different shape without it snapping. Metals are **ductile,** too, and can be pulled thinner and longer without breaking.

Physical Properties

Most **metals** have high **densities,** meaning that they are heavy for their size compared to other materials such as wood or plastic. Some metals are very dense. For example, a piece of tungsten the size of a large water or soda bottle weighs as much as an average adult person! There are a few metals with very low densities. For example, sodium can float on water.

Metal tracks carry electricity across this circuit board.

Metals and electricity

All metals allow electricity to pass through them, so we say they are good **conductors** of electricity. An electric current is made up of a moving electric **charge,** and in a metal the charge is carried by **electrons.** Some electrons from each **atom** are free to move from atom to atom and they move through a piece of metal, carrying the charge. Metals such as iron, copper, aluminum, and gold are used in electric cables and in electrical circuits inside machines because they help conduct the electricity.

In most **nonmetals** and **compounds,** the electrons cannot move, so they cannot conduct electricity.

Magnetic metals

A few metals are **magnetic,** meaning that they are attracted to magnets and can also be turned into magnets. For example, metal paper clips are attracted to a magnetic container. The most common magnetic metal is iron. The **alloy** steel is also magnetic because it is mostly iron. The two other main magnetic metals are nickel and cobalt. Magnetism is sometimes used in industry to sort metals during processing or recycling.

Radioactive metals

The **nucleus** of an atom is made up of **particles** called **protons** and **neutrons.** The metals uranium and plutonium have large nuclei with nearly one hundred protons and more neutrons, and some other metals have even more of each. A large nucleus like this is very unstable. Neutrons and protons often break away naturally, making it smaller and more stable. Metals like these are known as **radioactive** because as a nucleus breaks up, it releases **radiation** as invisible rays called gamma rays. Normally, the new nucleus has fewer protons, so the original atom is now an atom of a new, different **element.**

Experiment: Magnetic sorting

PROBLEM: How can we separate magnetic objects from a mixture of objects?

HYPOTHESIS: We can use iron's property as a magnetic metal.

> **EQUIPMENT**
> iron or steel nails
> copper nails
> magnet

Experiment steps

1. Mix up some iron or steel nails with some copper nails.

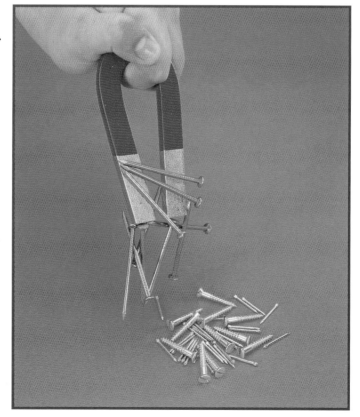

2. Move a magnet over the mixed nails.

RESULTS: Which nails does the magnet pick up? What do you think this shows about the properties of iron, steel, and copper? You can check your results on page 47.

Metals and Heat

All **metals** allow heat to flow through them. They are called good **conductors** of heat, meaning that if you heat one part of a metal object, the heat spreads quickly to the other parts of the object. This **property** of metals has both advantages and disadvantages. Cooking pans are made of metal because they conduct heat from the stove to the food inside them, but if you have a pan that also has a metal handle, you have to lift it with a pot holder or oven mitt to keep it from burning your hands!

Metals are good conductors because their **atoms** are closely packed together and strongly joined. The atoms in every material always vibrate because they have heat energy. The hotter an object becomes, the faster its atoms vibrate, because each one is getting more heat energy. When one part of a metal object is heated, the atoms in that part begin to vibrate faster because they are getting more energy. Some of this energy passes to the atoms nearby, making them vibrate too, and gradually the energy spreads through the object.

When atoms get more energy and vibrate more, they take up a little bit more space. This is why all materials, including metals, expand slightly when they get hotter and **contract** slightly when they get cooler.

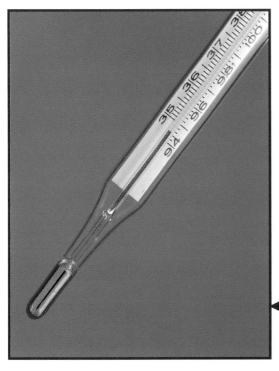

Melting and boiling points

All metals except mercury are solids at room temperature. Most of them have high **melting points** and even higher **boiling points.** For example, iron melts at 1,535°C (2,795°F) and boils at 2,861°C (5,182°F). Metals have these high melting and boiling points because their atoms are strongly joined together. Metals with very high melting points are used to make objects that are used in very hot environments, like inside jet engines.

Mercury trapped inside a thermometer expands when it gets warmer, indicating the temperature.

Experiment: Testing heat conduction

PROBLEM: Are metals better conductors of heat than plastics?

HYPOTHESIS: If heat spreads more quickly through metal than plastic, then it is a better heat conductor.

EQUIPMENT
peas
petroleum jelly
metal spoon
plastic spoon
mug

Experiment steps

1. Stick a pea onto one end of each of the spoons using a small blob of petroleum jelly.

2. Ask an adult to pour hot (not boiling or steaming) water into the mug, and stand the spoons in it. Make sure that the peas stay out of the water.

3. Carefully observe the petroleum jelly and the peas, and note the order in which the petroleum jelly melts and the peas fall.

RESULTS: Which pea fell first? What does this tell you about the conducting properties of metal and plastic? You can check your results on page 47.

Families of Metals

All the **metals** in the periodic table are found toward the left side. They are put into groups of metals with similar **properties.** Some of these groups are the **alkali** metals, the alkaline earth metals, and the transition metals. This section looks at these groups and the most important metals in each of them.

The alkali metals

The metals in Group 1 of the periodic table are called the alkali metals. They are lithium, sodium, potassium, rubidium, cesium, and francium. They are called alkali metals because they react with water to form alkaline **solutions.** For example:

$$\text{sodium} + \text{water} \longrightarrow \text{sodium hydroxide} + \text{hydrogen}$$

$$2Na + 2H_2O \longrightarrow 2NaOH + H_2$$

All the alkali metals are strongly **reactive,** and as you move down the group, the more strongly reactive they are. This means they are more likely to take part in **chemical reactions.** For example, lithium (at the top the group) fizzes slowly in cold water, but cesium (near the bottom of the group) catches fire instantly when it is exposed to cold air! Lithium and sodium have very low **densities** for metals and are very soft. All the alkali metals are silvery white in color. Because these metals are so reactive, they are rarely used on their own, but they have many useful **compounds.**

The alkaline earth metals

The metals in Group 2 of the periodic table are called the alkaline earth metals. They are beryllium, magnesium, calcium, strontium, barium, and radium. They are called earth metals because their compounds were first found in plant remains in soil. They also react with water to form alkaline solutions. For example:

$$\text{calcium} + \text{water} \longrightarrow \text{calcium hydroxide} + \text{hydrogen}$$

$$Ca + 2H_2O \longrightarrow Ca(OH)_2 + H_2$$

The alkali metal potassium reacts violently with water. The heat from the reaction ignites the hydrogen it produces.

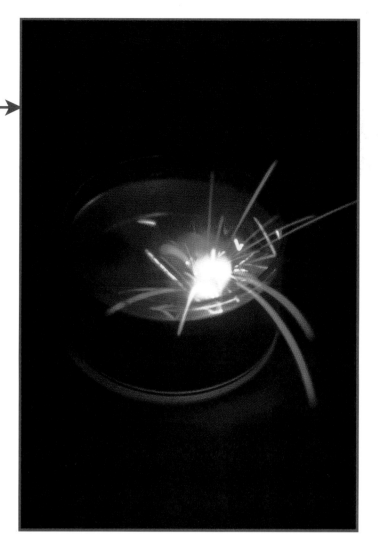

All the alkaline earth metals are very reactive, and as you move down the group, the more strongly reactive they are. For example, magnesium (near the top of the group) will react quickly with steam, but only very slowly with water, while barium (near the bottom of the group) reacts quickly with water. Most of the alkaline earth metals are silvery white in color. Like the alkali metals, they are rarely used alone, but they do form some very important compounds.

The sodium vapor that fills these lamps gives out yellowish orange light onto the lettuce seedlings growing below.

The Transition Metals

Most **metals** are in a large group in the center of the periodic table, in Groups 3 through 12. They are called the transition metals, and almost all of them are hard, strong metals with high **melting** and **boiling points** and high **densities.** The most commonly used transition metals are iron, copper, zinc, gold, and silver. Most of the other transition metals are very rare, yet scientists and engineers have found uses for many of them. They are mixed with iron, steel, or aluminum to make various **alloys** for engineering. Several, including palladium and platinum, are used as **catalysts** to speed up **chemical reactions** in factories.

Two groups of metals do not fit neatly into the periodic table and are sometimes left out and shown in a separate block. They are called the lanthanides and the actinides, and many of them have been made only in the laboratory. Many, such as uranium, are also **radioactive.** They are sometimes called the inner transition metals.

The transition metal chromium is used to make shiny parts for cars, and also to make stainless steel.

Gold and silver

Gold is the yellowish metal used to make jewelry and ornaments. It always stays shiny because, unlike most other metals, it is very unreactive—it does not react with the air to form a layer of **oxide** that spoils the shine. Gold is quite soft, so it is normally alloyed with other metals (usually copper or silver) to keep it from wearing away.

Silver is a whitish metal also used to make jewelry and ornaments. It gradually reacts with the air to form a brown layer of oxide. This process is called tarnishing, and it means that silver must be cleaned every few months. Many objects, including ornaments and cutlery, are silver-plated. This means they are made of steel with a thin layer of silver on the outside.

Metals in your body

Your body needs some metals for it to grow and work properly. For example, about two percent of your body is calcium, found mostly in your bones. Our main source of calcium as we grow is milk. There are other metals in our bodies in tiny amounts, including iron, zinc, magnesium, and copper.

It is important to eat foods that contain these metals. Some people take tablets, such as iron tablets, to provide them with these "trace" metals that are found in small amounts—or "traces"—in the body.

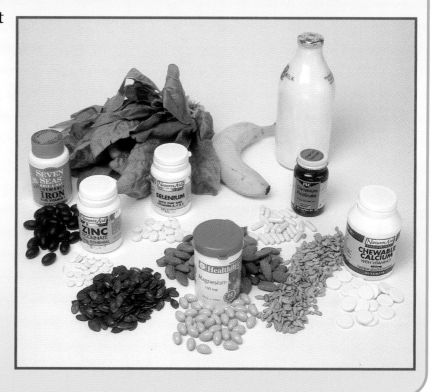

More Transition Metals

Iron is a transition **metal** and is one of the few metals that is **magnetic.** It is the most widely used metal of all. Pure iron is light in color and quite soft. Sometimes it is used to make decorative objects such as gates and railings. Blacksmiths work with iron by heating it to make it softer and then hammering it into shape. Iron is also made into large machine parts, such as cylinder blocks in engines, as well as objects such as drain covers and pipes.

Decorative gates and railings are made of a type of impure iron called wrought iron.

Iron is often made into steel, an **alloy** of iron and carbon. Most steel contains about 99 percent steel and about 1 percent carbon. Steel is stronger and harder than pure iron, but less **malleable** and **ductile.** It is good for making objects that need to be strong, so it is used in thousands of different objects such as cars, ships, skyscrapers, bridges, nails, screws, and knives and forks.

Iron and steel rust quickly in damp air. Stainless steel is an alloy of steel that contains about ten percent of chromium, another metal. The chromium keeps the steel from rusting, even if it gets scratched.

This decorative roof is made of copper. The copper's surface eventually turns green in damp air.

Copper

Copper is a soft, brown transition metal. It is a very good **conductor** of electricity, so it is used to make wires and cables. It is not very **reactive,** so it does not **corrode** in damp air like iron, and it is also easy to cut and shape. These **properties** make it ideal for making pipes for water supply and heating systems. Brass, used to make house fittings like door handles, locks, and screws, is an alloy of copper and zinc. Many coins around the world are made from copper alloys, too. The alloy keeps the color of the copper, but it is harder. Coins made from alloys last longer than plain copper ones would.

Zinc

Zinc is a soft, silvery transition metal. Its main use is for **galvanization,** a way of preventing steel objects from rusting. Zinc is also used in batteries and is alloyed with copper to make brass.

Other Metals and Metalloids

The remaining **metals** are in Groups 13, 14, 15, and 16 of the periodic table, although each of these groups also contains **elements** that are **nonmetals.** The metals are grouped towards the bottom and left of this section.

These metals are sometimes called poor metals because they are much softer and weaker than the transition metals. They also have lower **melting** and **boiling points.** The most important of these metals are aluminum, tin, and lead.

Aluminum

Aluminum is a silver-colored metal. It is the most abundant metal in the rocks of Earth's crust and has several useful **properties.** It is only about one-third the **density** of steel, but is just as strong when it is **alloyed** with small amounts of other metals. All large aircraft, and some cars and boats, are made from aluminum alloys. Aluminum is quite **reactive,** but its **oxide** is very unreactive. This means that a coating of oxide can form naturally on aluminum objects, but the oxide then stops any further **corrosion.** Most aluminum is made into soft drink cans and aluminum foil.

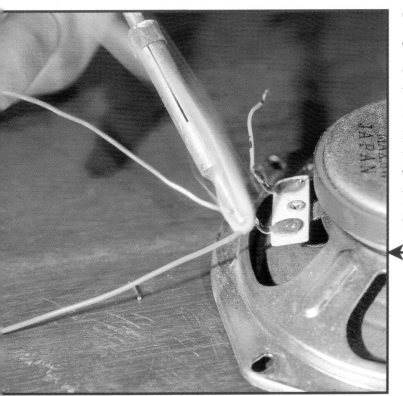

Tin

Tin is used to make a material called tin plate, which is steel with a thin layer of tin on one side. "Tin" cans are really made from tin plate, with the tin on the inside, next to the food. The tin keeps the steel from being corroded by the can's contents.

Solder is an alloy of lead and tin. The soldering iron melts it easily. It cools and turns solid again quickly, joining the wires together.

Lead

Lead is a very dense gray metal. It is used for waterproofing in buildings because it does not corrode. Thick sheets of lead block **radiation,** so it is also used to protect staff and patients in hospitals from **X-rays.** Lead used to be made into water pipes, but this was stopped because small amounts of lead were carried from the pipes into drinking water, poisoning it.

Metalloids

Most elements have either the properties of metals or the properties of nonmetals, although there are a few elements with some properties of both. These are called **metalloids** or semimetals. An example is the metalloid arsenic—it is shiny like a metal, but does not **conduct** electricity or heat. Silicon, the most common metalloid, is the second most common element on Earth's surface. Pure silicon is hard, shiny, and gray.

The most important use of metalloids is in making materials called semiconductors. A semiconductor is a material that can conduct some electricity but is not as good a conductor as metals are. This means it can be used to turn electric currents on and off. Microchips, often called silicon chips, are also made from silicon or other metalloids.

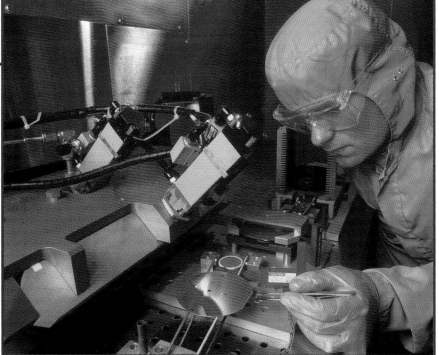

Silicon chips are made by building layers of semiconductors onto a wafer of silicon.

Metals and Air

The most common **chemical reactions** of **metals** are with air, water, and **acids.**

Iron or steel objects that are left outdoors quickly turn brown and flaky. This process is called rusting. The bright white flashes of fireworks are caused by the magnesium inside them burning. These are both examples of metals reacting with other substances.

Reactions with the air

Most metals react with oxygen in the air. The metal combines with the oxygen to form a metal **oxide.** Here is an example of a metal reacting with oxygen:

$$\text{aluminum} + \text{oxygen} \longrightarrow \text{aluminum oxide}$$
$$4Al + 3O_2 \longrightarrow 2Al_2O_3$$

This is an example of a type of reaction called an oxidation reaction. Oxygen is added to the aluminum, so the aluminum is oxidized. The evidence that the reaction has happened is that the shininess on its surface disappears—this is called tarnishing. The new aluminum oxide keeps oxygen from getting to the aluminum underneath. This prevents further tarnishing.

Some metals react with cold air. An example is sodium, a metal that is stored in oil because it reacts so quickly in the air. Some metals, such as magnesium, react only when they are heated. Others, such as iron, react only slowly, even when they are heated. Still other metals, such as gold, don't react at all—they are almost completely unreactive.

Exposed calcium reacts quickly with oxygen in the air to form a layer of calcium oxide.

Experiment: Metal and air reactions

PROBLEM: Do common metals react with the air?

HYPOTHESIS: Everyday metals such as iron, copper, and aluminum look shiny. They don't react with the air at room temperature, but they might when they are heated.

EQUIPMENT
thin strands of copper wire
thin strands of iron wire or
   steel wool
aluminum foil
tongs or a wood clothespin

Experiment steps

1. Cut a piece of aluminum foil about 1 foot (30 centimeters) long and 1/2-inch (1 centimeter) wide. Ask an adult to strip 2 inches (5 centimeters) of insulation from some stranded copper wire and some stranded iron wire.

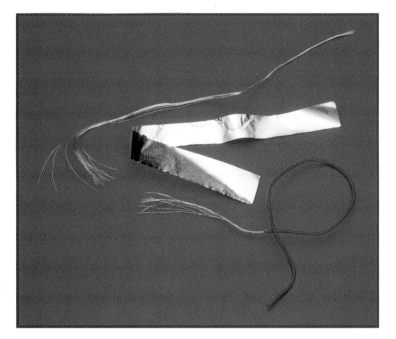

2. An adult must do this step for you. Ask him or her to heat the last half-inch or so (about a centimeter) of the foil in the flame of a gas stove until it glows red hot. Then remove it from the heat. Do the same with the iron wire and copper wire.

3. Allow the metals to cool for a few minutes and examine the parts that have been heated.

RESULTS: What do the metals look like now? What do you think caused this change? Which metal reacted most quickly, and what does this tell you about its place in the reactivity series? You can check your results on page 47.

Metals and Acids

Most **metals** react with **acids.** When a piece of metal is put into an acid, the metal fizzes because a gas is formed. This gas, hydrogen, is released from the acid. The metal combines with the rest of the acid to make a chemical called a **salt.** Here is an example of an acid-metal reaction:

magnesium + sulfuric acid $\longrightarrow$ hydrogen + magnesium sulfate

$$Mg + H_2SO_4 \longrightarrow H_2 + MgSO_4$$

The metal pushes out, or **displaces,** the hydrogen from the acid. This is an example of a type of reaction called a displacement reaction.

When different metals are added to acids, the fizzing happens at different speeds. When **reactive** metals, such as potassium, are added to acid, the reaction is so fast that the metal explodes. With other metals, such as magnesium, the fizzing does happen quickly but not explosively. When metals such as iron are added to acids, the fizzing happens slowly. Some metals, such as gold, don't really react with acids at all.

This magnesium ribbon produces bubbles of hydrogen as it reacts with hydrochloric acid.

Experiment: Reactions of metals and acids

PROBLEM: How can we remove the zinc from a **galvanized** steel nail?

HYPOTHESIS: Since zinc reacts with acids better than steel does, it might react with a weak acid, forming a salt and leaving the steel behind. Vinegar has a weak acid called acetic acid, so putting the nail in vinegar should work.

> **EQUIPMENT**
> galvanized steel nail
> white vinegar
> glass jar

Experiment steps

1. Pour an inch (2.5 centimeters) of vinegar into a glass jar. Vinegar is a weak acid, so be careful not to splash any in your eyes. Drop in a galvanized steel nail, and look at the nail every 30 minutes to see what is happening.

2. Wash the nail when the fizzing has stopped.

RESULTS: What happens to the nail after you put it in the vinegar? What do you think has caused this? You can check your results on page 47.

Metals and Water

Some **metals** react with water. When a piece of one of these metals is put in water, it fizzes because a gas is formed. The gas, hydrogen, is released from the water, and the metal combines with the hydrogen and oxygen in the water to make a hydroxide. This reaction makes the **solution alkaline.** Here is an example of a metal-water reaction:

sodium + water $\longrightarrow$ sodium + hydrogen
hydroxide

$$2Na + 2H_2O \longrightarrow 2NaOH + H_2$$

Some metals, such as potassium, react violently with water, and the reaction makes enough heat to ignite the hydrogen gas. Some metals, such as magnesium, react slowly with water, and others, such as copper, do not react with water at all. Some metals that don't react quickly with water, such as iron, will react with steam to make an **oxide** and some water.

A piece of potassium is reacting with the water.

The reactivity series

Different metals react with air, water, and **acids** at different speeds. In each reaction, the **reactant** and **products** are similar, but some metals react quickly while others react slowly. This is an example of a **trend**—it is always the same metals that react quickly and the same metals that react slowly.

We can list common metals in order of how quickly they react, with the ones that react most quickly at the top. The order is the same for reactions with air, water, and acids. Chemists call the list the reactivity series. Here is the reactivity series of common metals:

Metal	Symbol	Reactivity
potassium	K	Most reactive
sodium	Na	
calcium	Ca	
magnesium	Mg	
aluminum	Al	
zinc	Zn	
iron	Fe	
lead	Pb	
copper	Cu	
silver	Ag	
gold	Au	Least reactive

The reactivity series helps us to figure out what might happen during some **chemical reactions.** For example, a metal higher in the series will **displace** a metal lower in the series from a **compound,** like this:

copper sulfate + magnesium $\longrightarrow$ magnesium sulfate + copper

$CuSO_4$ + Mg $\longrightarrow$ $MgSO_4$ + Cu

Hydrogen is often included in the reactivity series as well. Acids contain hydrogen and will react with metals higher in the series, but they do not react with metals lower in the series. In the series above, hydrogen would be between lead and copper.

Corrosion

Corrosion is caused by a **metal** reacting with oxygen in the air, and sometimes with water or water vapor, too. We normally use the word corrosion when the reaction spoils and weakens the metal. Some metals, such as iron and steel, corrode quickly in damp air. Others, such as gold, don't corrode at all because they are very unreactive. Some metals, such as aluminum and zinc, do react with the air, but they do not corrode. This is because the metal **oxide** layer made by the reaction protects the metal underneath. This is why zinc and aluminum are used to make or cover objects that are outdoors.

Rusting

The most common form of corrosion is rusting. Rusting is the corrosion of iron and steel when they react with oxygen and water. The flaky, reddish brown rust is called iron oxide, and it crumbles away, allowing the metal underneath to rust, too. Here is an equation for one reaction that makes rust:

$$\text{iron} + \text{oxygen} \longrightarrow \text{iron oxide}$$
$$4\text{Fe} + 3\text{O}_2 \longrightarrow 2\text{Fe}_2\text{O}_3$$

The steel body of this van is gradually rusting away.

Preventing rusting

Rust on steel is an expensive problem, so it is important to prevent it. The easiest method is to cover the steel, keeping air and water from reaching it. This can be done with paint, plastic, or grease. Other metals that do not corrode, or that form protective oxides—such as zinc—can also be used. Covering steel with zinc is called **galvanization.**

Experiment: What causes rusting?

PROBLEM: What causes iron and steel objects to rust?

HYPOTHESIS: Iron or steel objects rust when they are left outdoors, but not when they are inside, so it is probably water or air, or both, that cause rusting.

EQUIPMENT
steel nails
4 glass jars
plastic wrap
calcium chloride (if available)
oil (such as cooking oil)
boiled water

Experiment steps

1. Stand four glass jars in a row and number them from 1 to 4. Drop a steel nail into each jar.

2. Pour an inch (two centimeters) of tap water into jar 1.

3. Fill jar 2 to the brim with water that has been boiled (by an adult) to remove dissolved air, and then cooled. Cover it with plastic wrap to keep air from redissolving into the water.

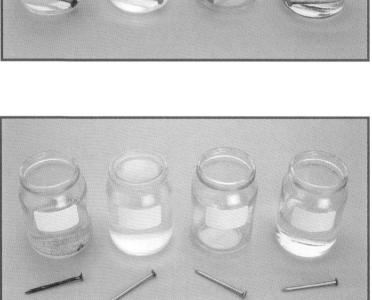

4. Put a few lumps of calcium chloride in jar 3. This will keep the air in the jar dry. If no calcium chloride is available, leave the jar empty, and put some plastic wrap over the top to keep damp air from getting in.

5. Fill jar 4 with enough oil to cover the nail.

6. Observe the jars each day for three days and write down what has happened to each nail in each jar.

RESULTS: What happens to the nails in each of the jars? What does this show about the effects of air and water on steel? Do you think both are necessary for rusting? You can check your results on page 47.

Finding Metals

All the different **metals** you see in ornaments, tools, furniture, buildings, and machines come from rocks that form Earth's crust. Before we can use metals, we have to find the rocks that contain them, dig them out, and then **extract** the metals from them. Some metals are abundant. For example, aluminum, the most abundant metal, makes up seven percent of the Earth's crust. Others are very rare, such as gold. It makes up only 0.0000005 percent of Earth's crust!

Metal	Percentage of Earth's crust	Date discovered
magnesium	2	1829
aluminum	7	1825
sodium	2.5	1807
zinc	0.007	2,000 years ago
iron	4	3,000 years ago
tin	0.0002	6,000 years ago
lead	0.0015	6,500 years ago
copper	0.0045	7,000 years ago
gold	0.0000005	10,000 years ago

This table shows the percentage of Earth's crust made up by the most common metals.

Metal ores

Most metals are found in **compounds** that are often metal **oxides.** These compounds are called **ores,** and they are normally mixed with the other compounds in the rocks. Mining companies find the rocks by conducting geological surveys. After the rocks are mined, they are crushed, ready for the metals to be extracted.

Very unreactive metals such as gold are not found as part of a compound. They are called **native metals,** and are often found in rocks as lumps called nuggets.

Extracting metals from ores

Metals are extracted from their ores using **chemical reactions.** In a reaction to extract a metal from its ore, the ore is one of the **reactants,** and the metal is one of the **products.** The higher in the reactivity series the metal is, the more difficult it is to extract from its ore. These metals are often more expensive to produce and to buy.

This copper ore has been blasted from a quarry.

Discovering metals

The discovery of different common metals through the ages is closely linked to the reactivity series. Gold and silver do not react easily and so are often found just as elements—that is, not combined in compounds. They were discovered more than 10,000 years ago. Copper was discovered next because it is only slightly **reactive** and can be extracted from its ore easily. It has been used for about 7,000 years. Iron is more reactive than copper and was discovered next, about 3,000 years ago. Aluminum is very reactive, so it is difficult to extract from its ore. Ancient people did not even know it existed, and it was not extracted until 1825, when the supplies needed to use electricity for electrolysis became available.

Extraction Reactions

The main methods of **extracting metals** from their **ores** are decomposition, displacement, and electrolysis. In each case, some energy must be supplied to break up the ore into its **elements.** All the methods of extracting metals from their ores are also known as smelting. For example, iron smelting is a process for getting iron from iron ore.

Decomposition

A decomposition reaction is a reaction in which a **compound** splits up to make two or more different elements or more simple compounds. This is called **decomposing**. Thermal decomposition is decomposition that happens when a material is heated. Mercury is extracted from mercury **oxide** by thermal decomposition. Mercury oxide is a red powder that decomposes when heated, making liquid mercury metal and oxygen gas.

mercury oxide $\longrightarrow$ mercury + oxygen

$$2HgO \longrightarrow 2Hg + O_2$$

Thermal decomposition works only for metals that are very unreactive. The ores of more **reactive** metals, such as iron and copper, would have to be heated to an extremely high temperature to make them decompose.

You can see mercury metal forming on the side of the test tube as heated mercury oxide decomposes.

Displacement

When a reactive metal reacts with the compound of a less reactive metal, the more reactive metal can **displace** the less reactive metal from the compound. The more reactive metal forms a new compound, and the less reactive metal is left on its own. These reactions are called displacement reactions. For example, if iron filings are added to a **solution** of copper sulfate, the iron (which is more reactive) displaces the copper. Iron sulfate and copper metal are formed as a result.

iron + copper sulfate $\longrightarrow$ iron sulfate + copper

$$Fe + CuSO_4 \longrightarrow FeSO_4 + Cu$$

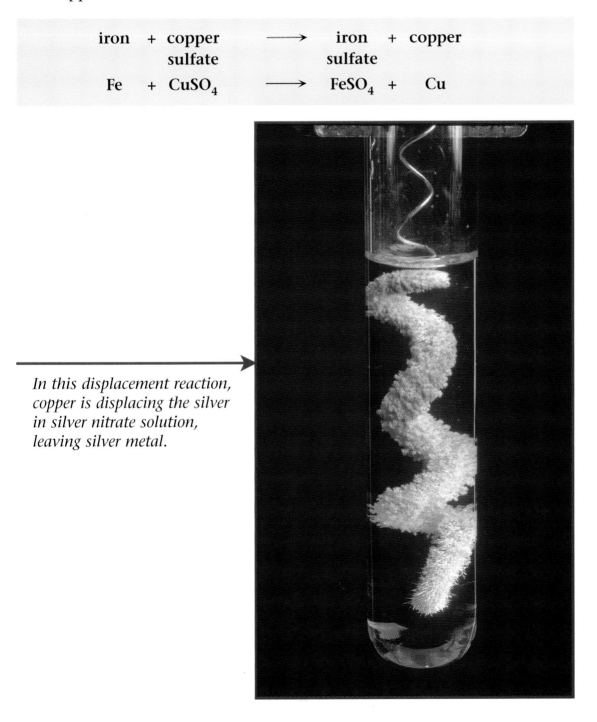

In this displacement reaction, copper is displacing the silver in silver nitrate solution, leaving silver metal.

Electrolysis

Electrolysis is a way of splitting a **compound** into its **elements** using electricity. It is used to **decompose ores** that would need to be heated to extremely high temperatures before they would decompose. Aluminum, magnesium, and sodium are all **extracted** from their ores by electrolysis.

Electrolysis can happen only to a substance that contains **charged particles** called ions. If an **atom** loses **electrons,** it becomes a positively charged ion, and if an atom gains electrons, it becomes a negatively charged ion. The substance must also first be **molten** to make a liquid, or dissolved in a liquid to make a **solution,** because the ions must be able to move freely.

To make electrolysis happen, two electrical contacts called **electrodes** are put into the liquid and then connected to a supply of electricity. This connection makes ions with a positive charge move through the liquid to one electrode, and ions with a negative charge move to the other electrode. When the ions reach the electrodes, they turn back into atoms.

Electrolysis is in progress at an aluminum smelting plant.

Extracting aluminum

The main ore of aluminum is bauxite, and it contains aluminum **oxide.** Since the aluminum in the ore is very **reactive,** it does not decompose when the ore is heated. This means it must be extracted by electrolysis.

First, the bauxite is processed to get crystals of pure aluminum oxide, called alumina. Alumina melts at a very high temperature that is too expensive to use, so it is dissolved at a lower temperature in a molten substance called cryolite. The mixture of alumina and cryolite is put into a container called a cell. The cell is lined with graphite, forming one of the electrodes. The other electrode, also made of graphite, dips into the mixture from the top. When electricity is passed through the mixture, aluminum ions are attracted to the graphite lining. They turn into aluminum atoms and group together to form molten aluminum. This is then piped off and cooled to form the finished **metal.**

Cheap aluminum

Scientists first extracted aluminum in the early nineteenth century, but only in tiny amounts, and the cost was very high. At the time, aluminum was in short supply and was more expensive than gold.

The most important breakthrough in the extraction of aluminum was the invention of the dynamo, a machine that produces electricity. This allowed power stations to be built, providing the electricity needed for the electrolysis of aluminum oxide.

Two scientists, an American named Charles Hall and Frenchman Paul-Louis-Toussaint Héroult, both developed a method of producing aluminum by electrolysis in 1886. Soon aluminum was widely available in large amounts, and became much cheaper than gold.

The Iron and Steel Industry

Iron is the cheapest and most useful **metal** in the world, and steel is its most important **alloy.** Iron-making and steel-making are two of the world's largest industries, and hundreds of millions of tons of steel are made every year for many different uses. Here you can find out how iron is **extracted** from its **ore** and turned into steel.

Smelting iron

Iron is extracted from its ore, iron **oxide,** in a very hot furnace called a blast furnace. Iron oxide and coke (almost pure carbon) are put into the top of the furnace, and air is blasted into the base of the furnace. The coke does two jobs. First, it burns in the air, heating the furnace to 1,500°C (2,700°F). Second, because carbon is more **reactive** than iron, it **displaces** the iron from the iron oxide. Here's the equation for the reaction:

$$\text{carbon} + \text{iron oxide} \longrightarrow \text{carbon dioxide} + \text{iron}$$
$$3C + 2Fe_2O_3 \longrightarrow 3CO_2 + 4Fe$$

The **molten** iron flows to the bottom of the furnace and goes through pipes to be collected. It is then put in molds and cooled. The iron from the blast furnace is called pig iron. It contains up to ten percent carbon, making it very brittle.

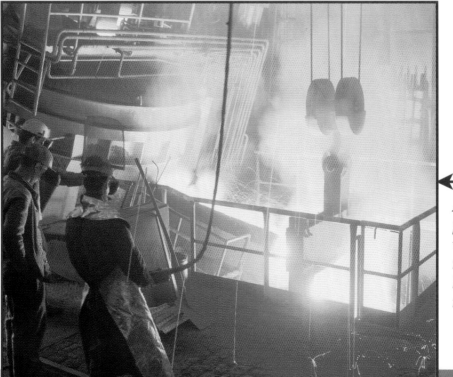

At this blast furnace, huge vats of molten metal are handled by remote control.

Iron to steel

Steel is iron that contains only about one percent carbon. Iron from a blast furnace is made into steel in a different furnace called a basic oxygen furnace. Molten iron is poured into the furnace. Then jets of pure oxygen are blown into the iron. The oxygen reacts with the carbon, producing carbon dioxide that is removed from the furnace. This reduces the amount of carbon in the iron and produces steel. The furnace is tipped up, and the steel pours into molds to cool. A large steel-making plant can make up to ten million tons of steel a year, or enough to make a thousand large cargo ships.

Henry Bessemer (1813–98)

British engineer Henry Bessemer invented the modern steel-making process in the middle of the nineteenth century. He realized that blowing air through molten iron would remove the carbon from the iron, making steel. Before this, steel was a very rare and expensive metal, but afterward it got much cheaper and became the most widely used metal of all.

Working with Metals

The **metal** made in most production plants is poured into molds to make lumps called **Ingots.** In a steel plant, the steel is fed into a machine that shapes it into sheets or bars. This is called continuous casting. Ingots, bars, and sheets of metal are the **raw materials** for making all sorts of objects.

Casting, forging, and rolling

Casting, forging, and rolling are the three main methods of making pieces of metal into different shapes. In casting, metal is heated until it melts and is then poured into a mold. Inside the mold is a hole the same shape as the object to be cast. The hole fills with metal that then cools, forming the object. In forging, the metal is heated until it glows red hot, but not enough to melt it. This makes it more **malleable,** and it can then be pressed or hammered into shape by machines or by hand tools.

In rolling, slabs of metal travel through a series of rollers that gradually flatten them into thin sheets, or bend them around into tubes. Blocks of metal can also be made into shapes with various cutting tools.

A blacksmith bends and shapes iron by heating it and hitting it with a hammer. This process is called forging.

Joining metals

Pieces of metals can be joined together by welding and soldering. In one method of welding, the edges of the pieces are heated until they are so hot that they fuse together. In soldering, used in electronics and plumbing, an **alloy** called solder is melted so that it flows into the gap between the metals, bonds to them, and joins them together.

Making metal coatings

Many metal objects have a thin coating of another metal on their surfaces. Eating utensils are often silver-plated, meaning they are made of steel with an outer coating of silver. Jewelry and ornaments are often gold-plated instead of being solid gold. Metal coatings are normally applied by electrolysis.

Metal recycling

Many metals can be recycled, meaning that metal in old or worn-out objects is made into new objects. Recycling not only saves more metal **ore** from being dug from the ground, but more importantly, it saves the energy that would have been used to **extract** the metal from the ore.

These aluminum cans are going to be recycled.

Metal fatigue

Metal fatigue happens when a piece of metal changes its shape a tiny amount, again and again. The metal weakens and eventually breaks. Metal fatigue is a big problem in machines where metal parts, such as springs, are stretched or bent again and again. This problem is difficult to detect, and parts often break suddenly, so it is important that parts of machines such as aircraft are checked regularly for the microscopic cracks that are a sign of metal fatigue.

The Periodic Table

The periodic table is a chart of all the known **elements.** The elements are arranged in order of their atomic numbers, but in rows, so that elements with similar **properties** are underneath each other. The periodic table gets its name from the fact that the elements' properties repeat themselves every few elements, or periodically. The position of an element in the periodic table gives an idea of what its properties are likely to be.

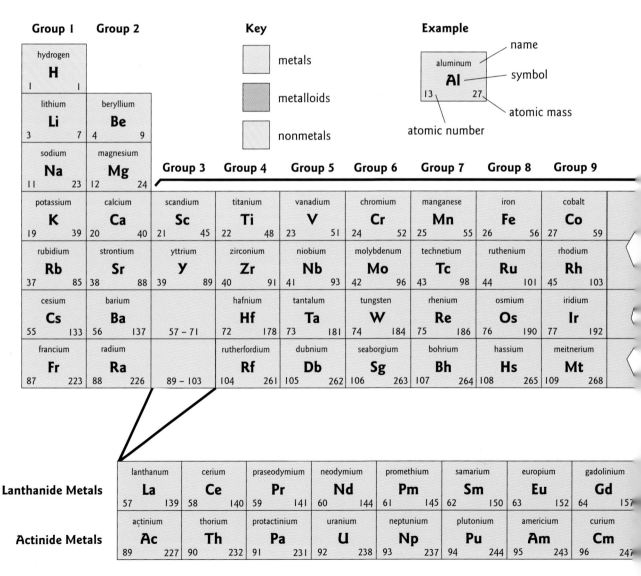

Key

- metals
- metalloids
- nonmetals

Example

aluminum — name
Al — symbol
13 — atomic number
27 — atomic mass

Group 1	Group 2		Group 3	Group 4	Group 5	Group 6	Group 7	Group 8	Group 9
hydrogen **H** 1, 1									
lithium **Li** 3, 7	beryllium **Be** 4, 9								
sodium **Na** 11, 23	magnesium **Mg** 12, 24								
potassium **K** 19, 39	calcium **Ca** 20, 40		scandium **Sc** 21, 45	titanium **Ti** 22, 48	vanadium **V** 23, 51	chromium **Cr** 24, 52	manganese **Mn** 25, 55	iron **Fe** 26, 56	cobalt **Co** 27, 59
rubidium **Rb** 37, 85	strontium **Sr** 38, 88		yttrium **Y** 39, 89	zirconium **Zr** 40, 91	niobium **Nb** 41, 93	molybdenum **Mo** 42, 96	technetium **Tc** 43, 98	ruthenium **Ru** 44, 101	rhodium **Rh** 45, 103
cesium **Cs** 55, 133	barium **Ba** 56, 137		57 – 71	hafnium **Hf** 72, 178	tantalum **Ta** 73, 181	tungsten **W** 74, 184	rhenium **Re** 75, 186	osmium **Os** 76, 190	iridium **Ir** 77, 192
francium **Fr** 87, 223	radium **Ra** 88, 226		89 – 103	rutherfordium **Rf** 104, 261	dubnium **Db** 105, 262	seaborgium **Sg** 106, 263	bohrium **Bh** 107, 264	hassium **Hs** 108, 265	meitnerium **Mt** 109, 268

	lanthanum **La** 57, 139	cerium **Ce** 58, 140	praseodymium **Pr** 59, 141	neodymium **Nd** 60, 144	promethium **Pm** 61, 145	samarium **Sm** 62, 150	europium **Eu** 63, 152	gadolinium **Gd** 64, 157
Lanthanide Metals								
Actinide Metals	actinium **Ac** 89, 227	thorium **Th** 90, 232	protactinium **Pa** 91, 231	uranium **U** 92, 238	neptunium **Np** 93, 237	plutonium **Pu** 94, 244	americium **Am** 95, 243	curium **Cm** 96, 247

Groups and periods

The vertical columns of elements are called groups. The horizontal rows of elements are called periods. Some groups have special names:

Group 1: Alkali **metals**

Group 2: Alkaline earth metals

Groups 3–12: Transition metals

Group 17: Halogens

Group 18: Noble gases

The table is divided into two main sections, the metals and **nonmetals.** Between the two are elements that have some properties of metals and some of nonmetals. They are called semimetals or **metalloids.**

Group 13	Group 14	Group 15	Group 16	Group 17	Group 18
					helium **He** 2 4
boron **B** 5 11	carbon **C** 6 12	nitrogen **N** 7 14	oxygen **O** 8 16	fluorine **F** 9 19	neon **Ne** 10 20
aluminum **Al** 13 27	silicon **Si** 14 28	phosphorus **P** 15 31	sulfur **S** 16 32	chlorine **Cl** 17 35	argon **Ar** 18 40

Group 10	Group 11	Group 12						
nickel **Ni** 28 59	copper **Cu** 29 64	zinc **Zn** 30 65	gallium **Ga** 31 70	germanium **Ge** 32 73	arsenic **As** 33 75	selenium **Se** 34 79	bromine **Br** 35 80	krypton **Kr** 36 84
palladium **Pd** 46 106	silver **Ag** 47 108	cadmium **Cd** 48 112	indium **In** 49 115	tin **Sn** 50 119	antimony **Sb** 51 122	tellurium **Te** 52 128	iodine **I** 53 127	xenon **Xe** 54 131
platinum **Pt** 78 195	gold **Au** 79 197	mercury **Hg** 80 201	thallium **Tl** 81 204	lead **Pb** 82 207	bismuth **Bi** 83 209	polonium **Po** 84 209	astatine **At** 85 210	radon **Rn** 86 222
ununnilium **Uun** 110 281	unununium **Uuu** 111 272	ununbium **Uub** 112 285		ununquadium **Uuq** 114 289				

terbium **Tb** 65 159	dysprosium **Dy** 66 163	holmium **Ho** 67 165	erbium **Er** 68 167	thulium **Tm** 69 169	ytterbium **Yb** 70 173	lutetium **Lu** 71 175
berkelium **Bk** 97 247	californium **Cf** 98 251	einsteinium **Es** 99 252	fermium **Fm** 100 257	mendelevium **Md** 101 258	nobelium **No** 102 259	lawrencium **Lr** 103 262

Common Elements

These are some of the **melting** and **boiling points** for pure metals and metalloids that occur in the periodic table.

Metal	Symbol	State at room temperature	Melting point (°C)	(°F)	Boiling point (°C)	(°F)
lithium	Li	solid	180	356	2,448	1,342
sodium	Na	solid	98	208	1,621	883
magnesium	Mg	solid	650	1,202	1,994	1,090
aluminum	Al	solid	660	1,220	4,566	2,519
silicon	Si	solid	1,414	2,577	5,252	2,900
potassium	K	solid	63	145	1,398	759
calcium	Ca	solid	842	1,548	2,709	1,487
iron	Fe	solid	1,535	2,795	5,182	2,861
copper	Cu	solid	1,083	1,981	4,703	2,595
zinc	Zn	solid	420	788	1,665	907
silver	Ag	solid	961	1,762	4,010	2,210
tin	Sn	solid	232	450	4,118	2,270
gold	Au	solid	1,063	1,954	5,378	2,970
mercury	Hg	liquid	-39	-38	675	357
lead	Pb	solid	327	621	3,171	1,744

The Reactivity Series

The reactivity series is a list of common metals in order of their reactivity, together with their reactions with air, water, and **acids.** The most **reactive** metals are at the top and least reactive at the bottom.

Metal	Symbol	Air	Water	Acid
potassium	K	Burns easily	Reacts with cold water	Violent reaction
sodium	Na	Burns easily	Reacts with cold water	Violent reaction
calcium	Ca	Burns easily	Reacts with cold water	Violent reaction
magnesium	Mg	Burns easily	Reacts with steam	Very reactive
aluminum	Al	Reacts slowly	Reacts with steam	Very reactive
zinc	Zn	Reacts slowly	Reacts with steam	Quite reactive
iron	Fe	Reacts slowly	Reacts with steam	Quite reactive
lead	Pb	Reacts slowly	Reacts slowly with steam	Reacts very slowly
copper	Cu	Reacts slowly	No reaction	No reaction
silver	Ag	No reaction	No reaction	No reaction
gold	Au	No reaction	No reaction	No reaction

Glossary

acid liquid that is sour to taste, can eat away metals, and is neutralized by alkalis and bases. Acids have a pH below 7.

alkali liquid with a pH above 7. Alkalis feel soapy and slimy.

alloy material made by mixing a metal with another metal or a small amount of a nonmetal

atom extremely tiny particle of matter. An atom is the smallest particle of an element that can exist and still have all the properties of that element. All substances are made up of atoms.

basic having the properties of a base, with a pH above 7

boiling point temperature at which a substance changes state from liquid to gas

bond chemical connection between two atoms, ions, or molecules

catalyst chemical that makes a chemical reaction happen faster but is unchanged at the end of the reaction

charge electricity on an object, such as an atom or electron

chemical reaction sequence that happens when two chemicals (called the reactants) react together to form new chemicals (called the products)

compound substance that contains two or more different elements joined together by chemical bonds

conduct to let electricity or heat pass through a substance

contract to get smaller

corrosion any chemical reaction that eats away a material, such as rusting

decompose to turn into more simple chemicals

density amount (or mass) of a substance in a certain volume. Density is measured in grams per cubic centimeter or pounds per cubic foot.

displace to push out

ductile able to be pulled into a thin wire without breaking

electrode solid electrical conductor, usually graphite or metal, that is in contact with the liquid in electrolysis

electron extremely tiny particle that is part of an atom. Electrons are negatively charged, and they move around the nucleus of an atom.

element substance that contains just one type of atom. Elements are the simplest substances that exist.

extract to remove a substance from a combination of substances

galvanization coating iron or steel objects with a layer of zinc to keep them from rusting

ingot piece of pure metal, such as gold, made by pouring molten metal into a mold

magnetic attracted to a magnet or able to be turned into a magnet

malleable able to be hammered into shape without breaking

melting point temperature at which a substance changes state from solid to liquid as it warms up

metal any element in the periodic table that is shiny, and that conducts electricity and heat well. Most metals are also hard.

metalloid element that has some of the properties of a metal and some of the properties of a nonmetal.

mixture substance made up of two or more elements or compounds that are not joined together by chemical bonds

molten heated to the point of melting

native metal metal that is found in Earth's crust as an element rather than as part of a compound. Gold is one example of a native metal.

neutron one of the particles that make up the nucleus of an atom. Neutrons are not electrically charged.

nonmetal any element that is not a metal or metalloid

nucleus central part of an atom, made up of protons and neutrons

ore material dug from the ground that contains useful elements such as iron, aluminum, or sulfur

oxide compound made up of a metal or nonmetal combined with oxygen, such as aluminum oxide or carbon dioxide

particle very small piece of a substance, such as an atom, ion, or molecule

product substance formed during a chemical reaction

property characteristic of a substance, such as color, feel, melting point, or density

proton one of the particles that make up the nucleus of an atom. Protons are positively charged.

radiation rays, such as light and heat, or streams of particles. Exposure to large amounts of radiation can be extremely harmful to people, animals, and the environment.

radioactive giving off radiation

raw material simple material that is made into more complex materials or objects

reactant substance that takes part in a chemical reaction

reactive taking part in chemical reactions easily

salt substance made when an acid reacts with an alkali or a base. A salt is always a compound that contains a metal and one or more nonmetals.

solution substance made when a solid, gas, or liquid (the solute) dissolves in another solid, gas, or liquid (the solvent)

trend general direction of change in a property

X-ray form of radiation that passes through some substances (such as flesh) but not others (such as bone)

Experiment Results

page 11: The magnet will pick up the iron nails but not the copper nails. This shows that the iron nails are magnetic.

page 13: The pea on the metal spoon is the first to fall because the heat from the water spread more quickly through the metal than through the plastic. This shows that metals are better conductors of heat.

page 23: Each of the metals you tested will be covered with a layer of a new substance. This is probably an oxide of the metal, formed by the reaction of the metal with oxygen in the air. The aluminum reacted most quickly, followed by iron and then copper.

page 25: After a few minutes, the nail begins to fizz. These bubbles are hydrogen being formed by the reaction between the zinc and the acid. When the fizzing stops, all the zinc has finished reacting, and a plain steel nail is left.

page 29: The only nail to rust is the one in jar 1, which was exposed to both air and water. This means that both water and air are necessary for steel to rust.

Further Reading

Blashfield, Jean F. *Iron & the Trace Elements*. Austin, Tex.: Raintree Steck-Vaughn Publishers, 2002.

Fullick, Ann. *Chemicals in Action*. Chicago: Heinemann Library, 1999.

Gardner, Robert. *Science Project Ideas about Kitchen Chemistry*. Berkeley Heights, N.J.: Enslow Publishers, Inc., 2002.

Moje, Steven W. *Cool Chemistry: Great Experiments with Simple Stuff*. Madison, Wisc.: Turtleback Books, 2001.

Oxlade, Chris. *Illustrated Dictionary of Chemistry*. Tulsa, Okla.: EDC Publishing, 2000.

Stwertka, Albert, and Eve Stwertka. *A Guide to the Elements*. New York: Oxford University Press, 1999.

Index